Love Me Gently

A Kid's Guide for Man's Best Friend

By Lisa Wiehebrink

Illustrated by Eleanor Harbison

For Henry and Jack, my greatest inspiration

ISBN-13: 978-1481026642
ISBN-10: 148102664X

Hi! My name is Henry and I am so excited because my family just adopted a new puppy. We named him Cooper. Having a puppy is fun, but there is a lot for both of us to learn. Most importantly, if I love Cooper gently, he will grow into the best dog ever and I will have a terrific friend.

Wow! Puppies sure eat a lot. Mom says it is because they are growing just like me. When Cooper is eating, I stay far away from him and his food bowl. He may think I am trying to take his food and growl at me or even try to bite me. That might hurt!

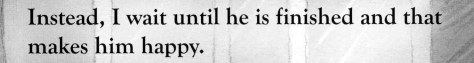

Instead, I wait until he is finished and that makes him happy.

COOPE

Just like me, puppies need to learn lots of new things. We are training Cooper to go potty outside. If Cooper makes poo poo or pee pee on the carpet, I don't get angry or scold him. That might hurt!

Instead, I patiently guide him where to go and that makes him happy.

Puppies are cute just like me. Cooper is soft and cuddly. He especially likes when I rub his fluffy tummy. I never pull his ears or tail and I don't squeeze him too tight. That might hurt!

Instead, I pet him tenderly and that makes him happy.

Just like me, puppies have lots of energy. Cooper loves to play, but he gets tired very quickly. When he is sleepy, I let him rest or even take a nap. I don't poke him to wake him up. That might hurt!

Instead, I wait until he is ready to play again
and that makes him happy.

Cooper has baby teeth just like me. Dad says he likes
to chew on things to make them feel better. Sometimes
Cooper takes my shoes and toys to chew on. If Cooper
makes the wrong choice, I don't hit him. That might hurt!

Instead, I give him his own toy or a puppy bone to chew on and that makes him happy.

Just like me, puppies are curious about the world around them. Cooper especially likes to go for walks in our neighborhood, but he moves a bit slow. I never pull him to go faster. That might hurt!

Instead, I walk alongside him letting him sniff and explore as we go and that makes him happy.

Puppies love to play just like me. Cooper likes when I toss a ball for him to fetch. I never throw the ball at him. That might hurt!

Instead, I toss the ball so he can run to get it and that makes him happy.

Puppies are fast just like me. If I leave our door or gate open, Cooper could escape and run into the street or even get lost. That might hurt!

Instead, I have to remember to do my part to keep him safe and that makes him happy.

Puppies are smart like me. They can even learn tricks. Cooper is learning how to "sit" and "stay". Sometimes he gets confused, but I don't shout at him. That might hurt!

Instead, I nicely ask again or gently show him what to do. I give him a yummy treat or a pat on the head when he does something right and that makes him happy.

Puppies need to eat special puppy food made just for them. I would like to share my favorite foods with Cooper, but it may not be good for him. It could even give him a tummy ache. That might hurt!

Instead, I make sure that he only eats his food and not mine and that makes him happy!

My family named Cooper for a very special reason. He wears a dog collar with a name tag at all times. If I take it off and he gets lost, he may not make it back home. That might hurt!

Instead, I always leave his collar on so that he will be returned home to my family and that makes him happy!

Just like me, Cooper is growing and learning every day. If I am kind, patient, and gentle with him he will become a well-behaved dog. Cooper is my best friend and a very special part of my family. He loves me as much as I love him and that makes us BOTH happy!

Lisa Wiehebrink grew up with a love of dogs and believes that pets can teach children important life lessons about compassion, kindness, and empathy toward animals and people. Her books are written to inspire children to be caring individuals and to empower them through age-appropriate responsibility. She is a dedicated animal advocate and a strong supporter of childhood literacy. Lisa is a Chicago native currently living in southern California with her family and four rescue dogs.

Eleanor Harbison used to draw elaborate stories on all sorts of scrap paper around the house as a kid. To this day, she loves telling stories through pictures. Eleanor enjoyed creating Henry and Cooper's world and illustrating their story, because she knows how her own childhood pets had a significant impact on her life. Eleanor lives with her husband, daughter, and son in Kansas City, Missouri.

Did you know...this book was donated by Tails That Teach, a nonprofit organization founded by the author Lisa Wiehebrink. Tails That Teach strives to empower young children with life lessons of kindness, compassion, and empathy by bridging the connection between people and animals.

Tails That Teach provides the books *Love Me Gently: A Kid's Guide for Man's Best Friend* and *Gray Whiskers: A Kid's Guide for Loved Ones Growing Older* to elementary schools and animal organizations across the country to encourage literacy and to facilitate compassion-centered programs that empower kids to be responsible for their actions and to respectfully care for others. When children are taught to be kind to animals, the ripple effects are boundless and children are less likely to abuse a pet or bully a classmate. By fostering the human-animal bond, children learn caring connections toward all living beings making a better future for animals and people.

Tails That Teach is also the proud founder of National Rescue Dog Day recognized annually on May 20 and dedicated to the extraordinary ways rescue dogs impact human lives while bringing awareness to the countless number of dogs waiting in shelters to be adopted.

To learn more about Tails That Teach, please visit www.tailsthatteach.org

Saving the lives of animals, changing the lives of children